Returning Home

An inspiring story of faith,
hope and love

Jeffrey Cole

Note for Librarians: a cataloguing record for this book that includes Dewey Decimal Classification and US Library of Congress numbers is available from the Library and Archives of Canada. The complete cataloguing record can be obtained from their online database at:
http://www.collectionscanada.ca/amicus/index-e.html
ISBN 1-4120-3854-5
Cover design by Mathew O'Malley.
Visit the author's Web site:
http://www.jeffreycole.com
First edition November 2004
Printed in Victoria, BC, Canada

TRAFFORD

Offices in Canada, USA, Ireland, UK and Spain
Book sales for North America and international:
Trafford Publishing, 6E–2333 Government St.,
Victoria, BC V8T 4P4 CANADA
phone 250 383 6864 (toll-free 1 888 232 4444)
fax 250 383 6804; email to orders@trafford.com
Book sales in Europe:
Trafford Publishing (UK) Ltd., Enterprise House, Wistaston Road Business Centre,
Wistaston Road, Crewe, Cheshire CW2 7RP UNITED KINGDOM
phone 01270 251 396 (local rate 0845 230 9601)
facsimile 01270 254 983; orders.uk@trafford.com
Order online at:
http://www.trafford.com/robots/04-1662.html

10 9 8 7 6 5 4 3 2 1

Author's Note

The true story told in this book is about many things.

It's the story about a simple and ordinary man who became extraordinary as he offered his family a glimpse into the world that lay beyond. It's the story about a man who struggled to come to terms with his life as time was running short. It's the story of his transition. It's the story about a daughter's devotion to her father during his final days on this Earth.

Most of all, it's a story about enlightenment and insight.

As my father-in-law lay dying in a nursing home bed, he worked tirelessly day and night to resolve his life, to understand his purpose.

At the same time, he worked to help his daughter and me understand the magnitude of what he was doing and where he was going. Our experiences were profound and life-changing. Our view of the world and our purpose here were forever shifted.

My hope in sharing this story is that comfort will be brought to anyone faced with saying good-bye to someone close to them. It is also my hope that comfort will be brought to those facing death. The world that lies beyond is real, and it's magnificent.

We received a rare gift of confirmation that there is a much greater existence than the physical world that we're so comfortable in and familiar with. We've come to understand that we all must find our meaning and purpose. We all must work to become enlightened and evolved.

When I embarked upon sharing this story, I believed that I had been given that glimpse into the other world because I had already spent much time in my life writing, which I believed enabled me to more easily write about our experiences. The reverse is actually true.

I've come to understand that I was given the ability to write so that I could share this story. My meaning and purpose are much clearer now.

As I believe our story will reveal, profound experiences do, indeed, happen to ordinary people. We must keep our eyes open and search for the greater meaning in the events around us. We must not dismiss what we don't immediately understand.

We must have faith.

To my father-in-law, Howard T. Bates.
Through him, I was given the two greatest
gifts anyone could ever receive.

Acknowledgments

So many forces came together to allow and encourage this book to be written. Some of them were of this world and some of them clearly were not. I am keenly aware that I was only the instrument through which this story could be shared, and for that, I am deeply grateful.

The support, encouragement and love of my wife filled me with the motivation and desire to share this incredible story. I am so thankful that we're sharing in this journey together, and I know that I'm blessed to have been able to recognize her when we found each other in this life.

My heart is full of appreciation for my grandmother, who left me all too soon, but who has continued to play an active role in my life. Thank you, Grandma Shirl, for staying with me. I look forward to our reunion.

Were it not for the unconditional love and support of my parents throughout my life, my heart would have not been open to allow me to truly understand the greater meaning in my father-in-law's death. Thank you both for your guidance.

A special thank you to my friend Linda Burnette, whose wisdom, insight and encouragement have also helped to guide me along the way. We have sorted through much together in our quest to find greater enlightenment.

Thank you also to my editor, Martha Friedrich, who has remarkable insight into the English language.

*Our eyes are holden that we cannot see
things that stare us in the face, until the
hour arrives when the mind is ripened...*

Ralph Waldo Emerson

Returning Home

Reunited in Death

I had wondered to myself for days how my wife would survive burying her father, mother and two grandparents in one morning. How would she get through it? How could I remain strong enough to help her? After all, that appeared to me to be my role — to make sure that she got through it. I could handle most anything, except to see that look on Audrey's face — that look of suffering. I had only seen it twice before this, once when she struggled with thyroid disease and once when her mother died. I was helpless then and felt helpless now.

Few words were spoken as we dressed. Even though we often discussed what we would wear to important events and usually sought each other's approval, this day was quite different. It was a day that we both were afraid of, each for different reasons and each on different levels.

I pulled a pair of black dress pants from our closet, knowing that black was the most appropriate color. A pressed white shirt, print tie and black loafers, and I had made the first decisions of the day. Would I be overdressed, I wondered to myself. I had never seen my father-in-law in anything other than black slacks, a short-sleeved dress shirt and a cardigan sweater. I had never seen him wear a tie. I wasn't even sure that he owned one.

This was a day to show my respect and love for my father-in-law. After all, he had given me so much during the past month. I must show him that he was important enough to me to wear a tie.

As Audrey sat on the edge of our bed and began to slip on a pair of black panty hose, I wondered if her father was beside her. She seemed a little stronger this morning. Her quietness told me that she was still deeply sad, but she seemed different in some way today. A little more at peace, like her father had been. Was he watching over her as he had promised he would just a week earlier? Yes, I believe he was.

After the journey on which he had taken us, this day should be a celebration of him. It should not be a day filled with sorrow, yet both Audrey and I felt a strong sense of dread. Neither of us had discussed our dread, but I felt mine and I could see hers. It was on her face and in her eyes. It joined the anguish that I had seen there for so many months. That beautiful, expressive face. She conveyed so much to me with her face and through her blue-gray eyes — so much I somehow understood but never pondered. Perhaps we had learned more about each other in the 10 years that we had been together than I had realized. Perhaps it was something even deeper — the understanding that you get of someone to whom you're so connected that words are unnecessary for communication.

As I watched her move slowly about our bedroom, she quickly became a blurred image of herself. My eyes filled with tears as her pain spilled over into me, and I turned and slipped into our walk-in closet to keep her from seeing me cry. It surely would unravel her to see me crumble, and I wanted to allow at least a few minutes of calm.

Don't let her forget what her father had given us, I continually reminded myself. Don't let her forget all that he shared. She especially couldn't forget it all today. He had worked so hard to ensure that she would be okay after he left. His work had been slow and methodical. He reached her soul in so many profound ways, and today was the day to begin remembering.

As I sat next to Audrey at the cemetery with my hand resting on her knee, I looked at the black panty hose covering her skin, and I again began wondering to myself. To find the panty hose in the middle of the floor of our closet a month earlier would have meant nothing to either of us. It probably would have given us reason to pause briefly, but wouldn't have seemed worthy of the time to ponder it. But now to find them there the day before when Audrey had walked into our closet to choose the right outfit for the funeral was not lost on either of us. There they lay on the floor, nowhere near where Audrey kept her panty hose. So many things had happened and continued to happen to us that were not of this world that we added that one to the list. Her father had already said so much, but he apparently wasn't finished speaking to us.

"I feel my father here with us," Audrey whispered to me as we stared at his casket. "I really do."

We sat in folding metal chairs, eye-level with the bronze casket sitting against the mausoleum wall in front of us, a flag neatly folded into a triangle and resting atop the closed casket. It was so much larger than I imagined that it would be. I was always surprised by the size of caskets, by the strength that they conveyed.

There were just six of us there to say good-bye — two of Howard Bates' three children, his sister-in-law, a niece and her husband, and me. Howard didn't have any close friends. He had been a very private man, and a very lonely man. I was never able to figure out whether his need for privacy prevented him from making friends or whether he was genuinely disinterested in other people.

Audrey's younger brother, Howard Jr., sat to her right, his shoulders slumped forward and his dark sunglasses hiding his emotions. Howie. He was always Howie to Audrey and thus was Howie to me. He was Howie to us and Howard to everyone else he knew. Howie seemed especially awkward on this day, not sure what, if anything, he was supposed to do. He seemed unsure what to do even with his hands. Perhaps they should be clasped in his lap, or perhaps one should be holding his sister's. He rested them in his lap. I was holding Audrey, having moved my right hand to her back. Howie sat alone. He had no one to hold him up, especially now that his parents were gone. He was 47 years old and his life had focused on his parents for much of those years. Before his mother died, she took care of him. After she was gone, his father took care of him. Audrey and I worried how he would take care of himself now that he was really alone.

To Howie's right sat Helen Wachholder —

their mother's sister. Aunt Helen was a sweet woman who adored Audrey and her brother almost as much as her sister had. She had recently turned 87, and while her mind was sharp enough to recall all of the recent events in her life, it was also still sharp enough to recall the 80 years that she had known her sister. Aunt Helen's hearing and vision had deteriorated, and she was unsteady on her feet. Her only child, Diane Young, was always by her side, holding her arm and leading her steps. Diane was there by her side this day also. Like her mother, Diane was a gentle, sweet woman who always put other people ahead of herself. She and Audrey had grown up near each other and had spent much of their childhoods riding bikes together, playing with their hula hoops and teasing Audrey's two brothers. Audrey and Diane had been best friends, and while they saw each other infrequently as adults, the bond between them was obvious when they reunited and recounted their memories as children.

Audrey and Howie's younger brother, Steven, should have been there with his family that day. After all, the three siblings had been so close as children. But so many days had already passed when Steven should have been with them that this day without him didn't seem unusual. Steven wasn't around when his mother died, so why should he show up when his father died? As far as he knew, they were both alive and well. I never actually thought of Audrey as having another brother. I had never met or talked to Steven, so it was easy for me to forget him when thinking of Audrey's family. Steven had lost interest in his family nine years earlier and dropped out of their lives. Howie had grown especially bitter that his brother was not around, perhaps because his brother wasn't having to feel the pain that he was feeling. He wanted his brother to hurt, just as his brother had made their parents hurt. Audrey had moved on, and while she had accepted Steven's departure, she still remained curious about his life and about him. She did still miss him, but she just learned to dwell on it less and less as the years passed.

The six of us sat in silence, looking ahead at the casket part of the time and at the three urns sitting to the right of the casket the other part.

Audrey's mother, Julie, had died six years earlier, and Howard had kept her ashes close to him. He couldn't let go of her. He left all of her things untouched in their home. He didn't get rid of anything. Her clothes still hung in the tiny closet in their bedroom, the folding door slid completely open as she had left it. The drawers of her dresser were still packed tightly. Her hairbrush and eyeglasses still lay atop her dresser, just where she had last placed them. Her white leather purse still sat on the floor by their bed. They had been so much in love, and all he had wanted for six years was to be reunited with her.

Two days earlier, his wish had finally been granted. Howard died on April 19, 2000, the same day Julie's father had died. They were the two most important men in Julie's life and both died on the same day, 52 years apart. The ashes of Julie's parents would be buried on the same day. Like Julie's ashes, those of her parents had never been buried. With all that we had experienced during the previous few weeks, we had come to understand that coincidences like these were much more than chance happenings. There was meaning and there was purpose, and we could no longer deny either. The key, we learned, was being aware and working to understand the meaning and purpose. Sometimes, it had been easy for us. Other times, it had taken days and weeks. But before Howard left, he made sure we understood all that was happening to him in his transition. He was patient with us, working throughout the day and night while we struggled to understand what he was telling us and what he was sharing with us.

After a few moments spent absorbing our surroundings, the funeral director appeared to my left, looking at me for some recognition that it would be okay to proceed. I smiled and nodded. As he walked between us and Howard's casket, I glanced up at his round face. David, I thought to myself; his name is David. It surprised me that I remembered his name. I wasn't usually good about remembering people's names. But his had stuck with me. He seemed so right for his job. He was quiet and gentle, his eyes filled with compassion. He must have been in this situation hundreds of times before. Yet he still managed to convey concern. He still managed to convey sincerity.

As David opened the casket and placed the square gold urn containing Julie's ashes next to Howard, leaves in the massive oak trees surrounding us began to rustle. A breeze suddenly picked up, and the air was cool and fresh. It was one of the few really nice days left before the summer heat settled over Florida. I took in a deep breath, filling my lungs. Audrey did the same.

Everything suddenly felt so good, so right.

"Can you feel that?" I whispered to her. "Can you feel the peace?"

Audrey smiled and nodded, tears streaming down her cheeks. She could feel it too. Her parents were most definitely together again.

It was symbolic, but it was good. It was very, very good.

Returning Home

Reunited in Life

Our journey had begun in March. At the time, there wasn't a noticeable beginning of anything. We were trudging through as we had for several months, watching a frail man become weaker, more tired and more frustrated. Our focus was on the ending that lay ahead, not the beginning of the journey we were about to embark upon.

Living alone for six years with only the grief that he felt since Julie died had taken a toll on Howard's health. She had died from congestive heart failure, all of her organs shutting down when her heart was no longer able to supply enough oxygen. It was the same condition that had slowed Howard so significantly. He had become a bitter and angry man, showing only occasional glimpses of a happier soul that lay smothered in self-pity. Our visits with him in the few years before his death had become short and infrequent, gathering mostly with him and Howie for holidays and birthdays. I came to dread the time with him and tried to find ways to keep the visits as brief as possible. I couldn't be around Howard for long periods of time because of the attitude with which he approached life. He complained about everything. Food was too expensive. Drivers had no consideration. Kids weren't being taught respect anymore. People didn't eat right. And on and on. There was no shortage of things to complain about. His mind and body had undergone major changes since Julie had gone.

Howard managed to live alone until shortly after he turned 82 toward the end of 1999. He had insisted on doing much of his own grocery shopping, paying his bills in person and picking up his own prescriptions. The dings and dents that began to appear on his gold Nissan Stanza were an early sign that he was having trouble living on his own, and we began to watch him more closely.

Audrey prepared soups, meat loaves, spaghetti and banana breads, leaving Howard to heat the food in his microwave. It wasn't long before she found the food was being left uneaten and he was losing more and more weight. Howie had begun running his father's errands, and the loss of independence devastated Howard. Depression set in. He had become unable to take care of his most basic needs, and his health needed more constant attention than he was receiving at home. He didn't have enough money for private, in-home care, and he didn't like having anyone in his home who wasn't part of his immediate family. He kept the orange curtains that had hung in the living room windows for more than 25 years closed, preferring to spend his time in the darkness watching television or just sitting quietly staring at the walls around him. He ventured outside only to retrieve his newspaper and mail. He had become a recluse with little connection to the outside world.

In early 2000, he recognized that he was too

weak to care for himself, and we found a room for him in a nursing home not far from his house. He agreed to be admitted. It was to be temporary, until he regained enough strength to enable him to again live alone.

Howard's first month in the nursing home had been filled with disappointment and anger. His muscles had deteriorated so much that he found it nearly impossible to muster the strength to build them back up again. Walking from his room through the nursing home and into the parking lot sapped his energy. He rarely had the strength for the return walk, so we rolled him back to his room in a wheelchair. He would lie back in his bed, exhausted. He wanted nothing to do with the other people in the nursing home, deciding that they belonged there and he didn't. His roommate was the exception, but perhaps that was because they lived just four feet from one another.

Paul was 82, a little round man who squinted when he talked. He was agreeable enough, but Howard complained that he was too nosy. As private as Howard was, he found most personal questions an invasion of his privacy. By Paul's account, his family had put him in the nursing home and had abandoned him there. While we didn't know his true circumstances, the fact that no one ever visited him seemed to confirm his story. Paul helped Howard pass the time, spending hours talking about baseball, my father-in-law's favorite sport. There was no team like his New York Mets. Win or lose, Howard was always a loyal fan.

While having Paul to talk to was cathartic for Howard, Howard was also terrified of him. His circumstances terrified him. While Howard had no plans to remain in the nursing home, he feared his family would abandon him there with Paul. Like Paul, Howard had lost much of his ability to care for himself, leaving him wondering whether he would ever return home.

He spent his days lying in bed, going on occasional walks only after our insistence. Seeing his health deteriorate after three weeks in the nursing home, Audrey and Howie decided he needed better care. They drove him to a nearby hospital, where he was admitted with pneumonia. He stayed there for the next five days.

His next and final stop was another nursing home, where Audrey had been able to arrange for a private room. It was to be temporary until he could become better able to care for himself again.

This time, he was more determined. He knew the key to getting home was in convincing his doctor, us and the nursing home that he could live alone. Only then could he return home. He worked tirelessly with a physical therapist exercising his legs and arms to rebuild his strength, and he worked with the nursing home staff to practice his cooking. He ventured out of his room to walk the halls.

But his body didn't respond as he expected it to, and he was unable to conceal his disgust. He lashed out at those around him, desperately searching for someone or anyone to blame. He became bitter. Nothing was going as he wanted it to. Nothing was going as he had planned.

He focused his anger on Audrey, Howie

and me, blaming us for locking him in an institution, stealing his home and his independence.

He had expected us to make him well enough to return home, and struggled with the realization that the effort had to come from within. With that realization came a more positive attitude as he again began the uphill climb to strengthen his body. He spent several hours each day exercising with a physical therapist, believing he could again care for himself and live independently.

After a brief improvement, his body began its final decline. We knew he would not recover. He knew he would not recover.

It was then that his real work began. It was then that our journey began.

Returning Home

The Turning Point

Although the turning point wasn't obvious at the time, and we weren't thinking of milestones that would be forever carved into our memories, looking back, we can easily pinpoint the moment that it all began.

It was a Thursday evening and Audrey had, as had become routine, stopped by to see her father after his dinner and before hers. She would usually spend a couple of hours in the evening with him before going home. The time together had become quite routine; he would complain that he didn't feel well and she would offer words of encouragement that often seemed lost on him. She would make sure that he had a full glass of orange juice for the evening, while also seeing if he needed anything else. For Howard, working his life back into some semblance of a routine gave him comfort.

That Thursday evening was very different than Audrey's previous visits. She noticed that he seemed much calmer, more comfortable and even happier. As he lay in bed with his head propped up on a pillow, a fluorescent light on the wall illuminating him from behind, he looked more content. He seemed pensive.

There were no complaints that night. Nothing was wrong. It was a very different feeling, and one that warmed Audrey. He was not only different from the previous few weeks, he was a different man than she had ever known. It was a change that she did not question and at the same time, did not understand. But, looking back, it was, indeed, a beginning.

"There's something I want to tell you," he had said, looking very deeply into Audrey's eyes. "You may find it unusual. You may not."

The words immediately made Audrey uncomfortable. She feared where the conversation would take them.

Howard then appeared to trail off, as had become common. He had begun to frequently forget what he was talking about. He knew his memory was failing, and he was frustrated that he couldn't recall where his thoughts were taking him. But this time, he was not searching for his thoughts. He said he was searching for the right words. It was methodical.

He went on to tell Audrey that her mother had been there to visit him that afternoon. That concept alone was not new. Howard had talked many times after Julie's death of having seen her. She had appeared at their home, in a vague one-dimensional image of herself, but never spoke to him. It had frustrated him that she wouldn't speak. But he had grown to accept it, somewhat satisfied that he at least was allowed to still see her. She would often appear in their bedroom from behind a towel that he had hung from a clothesline to dry. They strung the clothesline years earlier along one side of their bedroom, linking one paneled wall to another. The clothesline seemed strangely out of place in a tiny bedroom crammed with old mahogany furniture and a queen-sized bed. They were so accustomed to living simply that they never bought a clothes dryer, preferring instead to hang their wet clothes outside. When it rained, they used the line strung in the bedroom.

After becoming accustomed to seeing Julie appear and disappear from behind the towel, he hung an old wool blanket and more cotton bath towels over the clothesline to encourage her visits, hoping that privacy was the key to guaranteeing her visits. He had usually seen her accompanied by pets, first a dog and later a dog and a cat. The family never had a cat, and the dogs didn't resemble Bonnie, the Labrador mix they had in the 1960s, or Charkey, the small, black and gray terrier mix they had in the 1970s. The dogs didn't even resemble Beauty, the cocker spaniel that Howard and Julie got before their children were born.

We had never known whether to believe Howard or whether he might be hallucinating, perhaps conjuring up what brought him comfort. We knew we weren't equipped to judge.

In the nine years that I knew him, I never heard Howard talk of God, religion or the spiritual world. He didn't attend church and didn't read spiritual books. He clearly seemed focused on his life and physical being. That made his out-of-character stories of having seen Julie even more believable.

His usual focus on the present and what he could see, hear and touch was not unlike Audrey's and my approach to life. Although we had always believed in some higher power, it was not something we ever dwelled on or even discussed. Our lives were busy, and we left no time to ponder our purpose or meaning. We were skeptical of people who talked or wrote of experiences that were beyond this world and our understanding. Things needed to be explainable. Like Howard, we had chosen to focus our attention on our physical world, deciding we'd have plenty of time later to evaluate our ultimate fate. Audrey and I had never discussed attending church and had complained many times to each other about the hypocrisy of the religious people we had known. It seemed to us that this Earth and our lives were quite separate and distinct from anything that might follow.

As Howard continued that Thursday evening, he told Audrey that Julie had been three-dimensional during her visit in the nursing home that day. She also spoke to him and responded to him. He acknowledged how vastly different this experience had been from all of her previous visits.

Howard paused, looking across the tiny room that had become his home. His eyes searched the room. Audrey figured he had lost his thoughts. He again told her he was searching for the right words.

He continued, "I asked her where she had been. She told me she had been on a long mission, and she had come back to collect her things." Again he paused, searching the room with his eyes, pondering his next words.

"I told her everything was as she left it and to go ahead and take what she wanted."

He went on to tell Audrey that her mother had not been alone. There had been a dog with her. As before, it was not a familiar dog. Again he paused, allowing himself time to choose the right words. "I always thought you got to pick your own dog, but I guess I'll find out," he continued, in a matter-of-fact tone of acceptance and understanding.

Audrey listened to her father's words, trying to absorb all that he was sharing with her, but failing to grasp the meaning of the conversation. As Audrey and I would spend time over the next few weeks talking about and dissecting the powerful words that were spoken to us on so many occasions, our understanding would grow. We would become more enlightened.

Toward the end of their visit that Thursday, Howard made a statement that would remain in our thoughts for nearly every day until his death: "You and your brother will be getting the house on Thursday." The words drilled into Audrey, and she came to realize that their time together might be brief. She sat beside his bed, wondering whether he had some knowledge of the timing of his death. She wondered whether he had just a week left.

Howard drifted onto more mundane topics, pondering whether he had eaten dinner and what he might have eaten. The intensity and clarity with which he had spoken disappeared.

"Is it raining?" he asked Audrey.

Audrey moved over to the window beside his bed, gently spreading two slats in the white, metal blinds to allow her to see onto the courtyard. From the window, she could see across the oasis that was open to the sky and surrounded on all sides by the nursing home. A concrete path wound its way through the tropical plants and trees, and metal chairs sat empty for the night. It wasn't raining. It hadn't rained in several weeks and there was no rain forecast. If only it *would* rain. The plants in the courtyard needed rain. The worst drought in more than 25 years had settled in, and there was no rain on the horizon.

"No, Dad, it's not raining."

She sat with her father for a while longer, talking of little as she thought of the vastly different feelings in the room that night. She couldn't immediately pinpoint it, but she knew there was something suddenly so nice about being there. He was a calmer and more positive person than she had ever known.

28

She kissed her father good-bye, maintaining her strength and fighting back the tears as she told him she loved him. Leaving the room, tears began to stream down her face as she began to miss him.

As she stepped outside, she realized her father was speaking to her on a different level now. The skies suddenly opened up and rain was falling to the ground. He knew it was about to rain, she thought. He knew it and he wanted me to know he knew it, she said to herself.

Returning Home

A Higher Level

Two days later, I joined Audrey for a visit with her father. I was curious about the changes in him that Audrey had described, and was equally curious about the positive feelings that Audrey had being with him. For the first time in several years, I was eager to spend time with him. I wanted to understand what had changed and why changes were happening.

The visit began like many of the others. We greeted one another and he proceeded to talk about how bad the food was. He would describe the food in a level of detail that allowed me to fully appreciate that the food was, indeed, bad. The gray roast beef tasted like it looked, and the hamburger goulash macaroni surprise could not be adequately described. We settled in to watch television together, a pastime that he deeply loved and one that had been integral to his routine at home. To have us there to share that experience with him helped, I believe, to make his day complete.

Howard had never played golf, but enjoyed watching it on television, as he did that Saturday afternoon. He was reclined in his bed with two pillows under his head. I sat to his right in a blue vinyl chair with wooden arms and a high back, both of us facing the television which sat on a shelf across the room just below the ceiling. Audrey sat in the corner across from me and under the television, leaning against Howard's navy blue cardigan sweater hanging over the back of the chair. The vinyl recliner that she sat in was positioned in front of a French door that swung out into the courtyard. The blinds on the door and on the window to the left of the door were cocked open enough to let light in while keeping the hot rays of the sun out.

Howard's twin bed took up most of the

room. The narrow areas on either side of the bed provided enough room for matching two-drawer wooden tables, with a collection of medications, ointments, sugar packets, straws and Styrofoam cups scattered across their surfaces. He loved to save whatever he did not use during a meal, and his sugar packets became his most expansive collection. Two pairs of polyester black pants hung in a closet recessed into the wall to his right, along with several plaid, short-sleeved dress shirts. In the drawers below the closet were his black socks, white boxers and white undershirts. His black sneakers with Velcro straps were neatly placed under his bed, his wooden cane dangling from the side of the bed just above his shoes. Seeing the sneakers sitting there day after day reminded me of the brown Velcro sneakers that his wife had worn on her last trip to the hospital. Waiting to make the arrangements for her cremation, I had watched the funeral director walk in and place her pants and blouse on the table beside Howard. He then placed her brown shoes on top of the pile. Howard stared blankly at the shoes, not knowing what he was supposed to do. She seemed really gone at that moment.

As I stared up at the television screen, my mind wandered to the change that was so obvious in the room and in Howard. It was difficult, actually impossible, to understand. I just knew that it was no longer a depressing place. It was suddenly comfortable and soothing. There was a warmth.

I was unable to concentrate on the television as I allowed myself to experience the changes around me. I could see his eyes tracking around the room. His face suddenly took on an inquisitive and intense look, and it was obvious that he was focused on something. It was nothing that I could see, but it felt as though the three of us were no longer the only three in the room. Energy was all around us. Something had begun to occur beyond what my eyes were allowing me to see, but that somehow I could feel.

Afraid that he would see me staring at him, I glanced back at the television. As I stared blankly ahead, my mind filled with thoughts of Howard, his voice and his words. I could hear his voice as though he were speaking to me from his bed, yet there was no audible sound.

"You're fixing up my house so you can sell it," I could hear him saying. I was puzzled by the sound of his voice because I heard nothing through my ears. My thoughts went on to reassure him that I was interested only in his well-being. Audrey, Howie and I had spent a day cleaning the inside of his house and having his leaky roof replaced in preparation for his return home. That was the truth as I thought I knew it then. Looking back, I knew that he wouldn't return to his house, and I was, indeed, preparing it to sell after he died. He was more aware of that truth at the time than I was.

I shifted my thoughts to what was happening to him and where he was going. I thought about how badly I wanted to see what he was seeing, how badly I wanted to experience what he was experiencing. There was no response. I had never had an experience communicating with someone in my mind, and I doubted that I was experiencing such a phenomenon then.

Perhaps I was wanting Howard to communicate with me on some level beyond the obvious and familiar one. Or perhaps I just wanted to believe it was possible. Perhaps I felt guilt over his house and manifested the conversation as a way to rid myself of the guilt. Whatever was happening, it did strike me as odd that his voice had appeared in my mind so suddenly.

While I doubted myself, I also began to marvel at the possibility. I needed proof. I needed a sign, any tangible sign, that what I was experiencing was real. In my thoughts, I told my father-in-law that I would turn to look at him and that I wanted him to look back at me at the same moment.

My heart pounding, I slowly turned my head toward him. As I did, he slowly turned to look at me. He stared more deeply into my eyes than anyone ever has, fixing so strongly on me that it made me uncomfortable. As he stared at me, a wide smile came across his face. He grinned with a look of recognition that Audrey later said looked as though we were sharing something. Indeed we were.

The intensity of his stare bore into me so strongly that I had to look away after a few seconds. Looking back at the television, I worked to resume the connection. I was speaking to him in my mind, but he wasn't there. A nurse came into the room and he focused on her. As hard as I worked later during that visit and in future visits, I never experienced that type of communication with him again. Our communications would move to an even higher level. I had gotten the first part, and we would continue moving forward until I got it all.

Returning Home

Life Before Death

Driving west down the two-lane road that divided the rural Florida town's old concrete block one-story homes from the contemporary one-story stucco homes always gave Audrey and me pause to think about what might be next in our lives. The silence in the car was never uncomfortable because our minds were grinding through the past, present and future as we drove to the nursing home. As my eyes skipped across the mildew-stained rooftops along the south side of the road, I wondered what my thoughts would be on the return home down this same road. Audrey stared out at the north side, barely able to see through the thick brush that had grown up along the road. She thought of her father lying in bed, looking less and less like the man she had always known.

His body looked pathetic, and it hurt her to see him so weak. Although she wanted to care for him, it hurt her most that she had to. This was her father, the one who was supposed to be in charge and in control.

Audrey's new role in her father's life brought back some of the strongest and most stirring memories from her childhood. Her mind roamed back 35 years. She was 15, and she and her family were living in Queens, New York. She had just come home from school with an upset stomach and diarrhea. Within several hours, she became sicker as her two brothers became nauseated and they, too, began having diarrhea. Their mother was in St. Johns Hospital recuperating from a hysterectomy. Howard fixed Audrey and her brothers dinner, but they were too sick to eat. Audrey recalled being saddened that her father had gone to the trouble to fix them a dinner that they were unable to eat. At 9:30 that night, Howard set out on foot to buy syrup of cola at a nearby candy store to soothe their stomachs.

Audrey became frantic after her father had been gone for 45 minutes, and she headed out to find him. Just a block from their house, she doubled over in pain, more worried about her father than her own illness. As if from nowhere, her father appeared, lifted her into his arms and carried her home. He was always there to help her and comfort her.

Now, it was her turn to comfort and care for him.

Audrey visited her father every day, usually twice each day. She struggled within herself over his decline, not wanting to see him suffer but not wanting him to leave her. As he lay in bed, she doted on him, fetching anything and everything that he needed or wanted. She dabbed his face with a warm, moist cloth. She helped him urinate.

Helping him use a urinal in bed, standing over him and helping to make sure that he didn't soil himself or the bed as he used the urinal, had been his most dramatic relinquishing of control and dignity. For a man who had been so modest and private that he always wore socks and long pants even around his family at home to now allow his daughter to help him on such a personal level said a lot about the stage of his life and the bond with his daughter.

She would sit for hours holding his hand, caressing his head, comforting him with her smile. She wanted to make him better, but she would settle for making him feel better.

As we turned into the parking lot, the pine trees towering over the one-story nursing home always caught my eye. They were so beautiful, so natural and so untouched by human suffering. The empty parking spaces on either side of the two to three parked cars always caught my eye after I saw the pine trees. At least there were some cars in the parking lot, I thought. At least someone is being visited. Perhaps the home is as frightening to others as it had been to me.

Initially, we preferred to spend our time in Howard's room, blocking out as much of the incoherent ramblings of some of society's forgotten as we could. During the days, elderly men and women sat in wheelchairs and small school desks crowded around a nurses' station located in the center of three hallways that came together. Some cried out for help, seemingly unaware of what they needed or wanted. Others moaned, or babbled unrecognizable words and sounds. Still others sat quietly, absorbing the movements and life around them.

Some were missing limbs, and others looked so frail that I wondered how they were still drawing breath. Some twitched uncontrollably.

It scared me to look at them. It scared me more when they looked at me. I avoided eye contact, not even looking in their direction when they called out to me.

The more mobile residents wandered the hallways, some aimless in their movements and others quite aware of their surroundings. *Awakenings* played through my head at some point during each visit. It was a movie that Audrey and I had watched together three or four times. The tragic true story that it told of people trapped within their own bodies, unable to respond, had always amazed and horrified us. It was almost too unbelievable to be believable. Why was life reduced to this, I wondered. This is where people are delivered to die. Will this be my future?

In the weeks that we spent there, we had come to understand some of their patterns of behavior. We learned who was easy to communicate with, and who was not.

Three stood out, and, ironically, the three were among those who initially made us most uncomfortable. Their struggles seemed intense, and all three allowed us to move beyond the words we rely on to communicate. Like my father-in-law, they brought us into their souls, ultimately communicating with us well beyond our verbal, human world.

Conrad was a pathetic sight. Nearly 90 years old, he was thin and frail, his wrinkled cheeks sunken and his thin white hair always looking as though he had just lifted his head from a pillow. He spent much of his time wandering the hallways in a wheelchair. His feet did all of the work while his arms rested on his lap or on the arms of the wheelchair. He looked tired and worn. Although he seemed to understand his surroundings, communication was fairly limited. I felt thankful that I could understand my father-in-law and that he could understand me.

Conrad seemed the same every time we saw him. We watched him slowly make his way down the halls, sometimes steering into walls and struggling to right himself. We helped him when we could, but there was no conversation and no recognition in his eyes.

Navigating his wheelchair seemed to become easier when we noticed him sporting a pair of new gray sneakers. Walking into the home one day and seeing only those sneakers lying in the middle of the foyer brought a smile to our faces. Such an amusing, yet sad, sight. As we walked by his room, Conrad lay asleep in his bed.

The woman we came to call The Clapper was more unsettling and far less amusing. She spent much of her time sitting in the foyer clapping at anyone who walked by while yelling "Hey!" She had a toothless grin and a wild look.

Diminutive Peggy seemed the sweetest and most frail of the three. Standing about 5 feet tall with a waist that couldn't have been more than 20 inches around, Peggy reminded me of Audrey's mother. They both had full heads of thick, wiry gray hair, although Peggy's was far less in control, leaving her looking as though she had just been electrocuted. Peggy sat at the nurses' station fiddling for hours with plastic bags or randomly turning the pages of books. She was quiet and kept to herself, focusing her attention on whatever was directly in front of her. I walked by her many times, yet she never looked up at me. She didn't appear aware of anything going on around her.

The Work

Howard's behavior continued to change with each day that passed. He began talking in his sleep. He would ramble on to himself for much of Audrey's visits, his facial expressions changing frequently as he lay in bed. At times, he looked quite elated; at other times, his face would contort to reveal that he was deeply disturbed and upset. While he was asleep, he talked about Julie, his dead brother and five dead sisters. He would move his hand back and forth at his side just above the bed as though he were petting a dog. He would reach out as if to embrace someone, moving his lips as though he were greeting them with a kiss. He would return his hands to his chest, interlace his long, bony fingers, a smile always sweeping across his face after an embrace and greeting.

He seemed to carry on conversations with those he greeted. As he greeted people, we would only understand the names and the greetings. Sometimes he would smile and say hello, and other times he would ask them, "How are you?" After the greetings, he would begin mumbling, which allowed us to understand only some of his words. He seemed comfortable with those he spoke with, and the warmth of the greetings seemed to be what I'd expect from a relative I hadn't seen in a year. Although some of the relatives he greeted had been dead for several decades, there wasn't an exuberance of having been reunited after that long. Their time apart seemed much shorter.

Sometimes his talking was not preceded by greeting anyone, but he always seemed to be talking with someone. He spoke of his time overseas in World War II, mentioning his rifle and "the pretty girls" with a grin on his face, his eyes remaining closed. From pictures taken during the war that we would later find hidden under a dresser in his house, it appeared that, as a young man in the Air Force, he hadn't been quite as inhibited as he became later in his life. Crumpled black-and-white pictures captured him and his friends sitting in strip clubs, as large-breasted naked women paraded on stages in front of them. It was a rite of passage for men during that war.

While asleep, he spoke of the dead. While awake, he mostly spoke with us about the living. Julie was the only exception. He spoke of her while asleep and awake.

Between naps, he reminisced with Audrey about trips the family had taken between New York and Florida, the cities he had visited in Italy during the war and the things they had done as a family. He asked about the weather. He talked about wanting to go home to be with their family.

His eyes often tracked around the room. We observed him carefully, watching him frequently fix his stare on one area of the room, a look of awe often sweeping across his face. He had begun to talk about the hard work that he was undertaking, but failed to explain anything further to us. We didn't ask questions, somehow understanding that he would share what needed to be shared when it needed to be shared.

He began to mention his "work" so frequently to us that we spent much time pondering the meaning. Initially, we attributed the "work" to confusion. Perhaps he was dreaming of years before when he had worked as a carpenter. Perhaps he was having trouble distinguishing between past and present. As the talking in his sleep became nearly continuous and his facial expressions reflected greater and great consternation, it became obvious to us that there was, indeed, a great deal of work involved in whatever was happening to him.

As the first Thursday arrived since he had spoken of Audrey and her brother getting his house on Thursday, Audrey awoke especially troubled. It was a much greater effort getting out of bed that morning, but she found some comfort in her own routine. Weekdays were always the same: a one-mile walk every morning at 5:30, followed by a shower, a breakfast of oatmeal and decaffeinated coffee, and a seven-minute drive to work. She allowed herself to sleep until 6 a.m. on the weekends, and added a mile to her walk. But the routine was nearly identical every day. Like her father, Audrey loved structure and routine. Working for the same county government for 27 years allowed her to develop close relationships with colleagues who were comforting to be around during the previous few months. She needed familiarity. There was no denying that she was her father's daughter.

Sitting at her desk in a cubicle by a door leading into a hallway on the first floor of one of five government buildings in the complex where she worked, a charge shot through her every time the phone rang. With each ring, her heart raced, as she feared she might receive the call that she dreaded.

Audrey visited her father during her lunch break that day as she did every day, making sure that he was comfortable and fed. She found him troubled and emotional on this Thursday.

He asked about his bills and finances, a

look of shock sweeping across his face when Audrey told him he had about $10,000 in his bank account. It was more money than he could fathom. He had been short on money throughout his adult life, and to him, $10,000 was a fortune. Audrey explained that because of his health, the Department of Veterans Affairs had agreed to increase his monthly checks. She had fought for money owed him for the past several years and put it all aside for his care.

"All of that money is for you, Audrey."

"No, Dad, it's your money."

Howard continued to insist that whatever money he had was hers. The conversation felt morbid to her; she didn't want either of them to hasten his death by dividing his assets. She found an end to the conversation: "Look, Dad, are we going to have to go out into the parking lot and rumble?" Howard had always felt that humor was a valuable characteristic, and he was proud that his daughter had inherited his sense of humor. He returned her smile, realizing that his only daughter and oldest child had no plans to back down in this conversation but feeling that his point had been made. It was a rare moment in their relationship. Despite how difficult a man Howard could be, Audrey had adored her father throughout her life, as daughters do. She had enjoyed spending time with him for more years than she didn't, and at this point in their relationship, she was noticing changes in him and in them. Difficulties between them were fading, and the memories that brought her happiness were flooding into her consciousness.

As she sat with her father, she drifted back to being 10 years old again. She had often insisted on accompanying him to carpentry job sites. Dressed in jeans and a T-shirt, she loved to stand for hours and watch her father work, handing him the tools of his trade as though she were a nurse in an operating room. She learned much about him and about carpentry during that time together.

But she had also feared her father. She had navigated through their relationship and the others in her life focusing great energy on avoiding upset and conflict. She acquiesced whenever necessary to ensure that he was not upset with her. She could not bear her father's disapproval.

Howard shifted the conservation to his surroundings, complaining about living in the nursing home. As he expressed his desire to go home, he began to cry. Audrey had seen her father cry only once before. It had been six years earlier when her mother died. He was becoming more sensitive, more gentle, more vulnerable. He had begun to occasionally ask Audrey how she felt, how she was coping. He had suddenly become far more concerned with his daughter's welfare than he ever seemed to be before. That shift was in sharp contrast to the entire time she had known him, when much of the family focused its attention on him and his needs. He was, indeed, changing. It was an evolution.

As Audrey left his room that Thursday afternoon, wondering if she would see him alive again, she kissed him and told him that she was leaving a box of tissues on the bed beside him. "Oh, Audrey, I won't be needing those," he told her. "I've got a lot of work to do this afternoon." He turned to look straight ahead and closed his eyes, returning to the "work" that had become so important.

In the next two weeks, the intensity of that work became apparent. He stopped eating and preferred to be left alone to sleep. Although at first glance it appeared to be sleep, what was occurring during those periods was not restful. He struggled and he worked. His window of opportunity did not appear to be wide, and it seemed that he had much to accomplish.

We feared that his not eating would hasten his death, that he would become ill. "His body doesn't need food now to sustain itself," a nurse said to us.

Returning Home

Time to Say Good-bye

Audrey returned again that Thursday evening to find her father looking intense. She had not been there long when he looked at her and said, "I'm dying." Although doctors had told Audrey that her father likely had several more months, if not a year or more left in his life, the realization that his time would be much shorter was one that Audrey had come to understand in the previous few weeks. But hearing her father say the words, to acknowledge the fact, hurt. She held his hand and nodded in agreement.

"I don't understand what it's all been about, but I guess I'll find out," he continued. The words hung in the air as Audrey let her father speak, cupping his left hand in both of hers.

"Are you okay?" he asked, fixing his stare on her eyes. She smiled, "I'm fine, Dad." But she wasn't fine. She wasn't prepared to let go of her father and the connection that he provided to her mother. It was too soon. She needed more time. She could feel the bond between them growing stronger with every hour that they were together.

He knew what she needed, and he wouldn't go until he was sure she was ready.

During the next week, Audrey and her father would share more memories than they had talked about during the past several decades. She would sit with him for hours caressing him and holding him. She thanked God for the time they'd been given. She begged for his suffering to end and at the same time begged for more time together.

While it was clear that Audrey was adjusting to the idea that she would soon be without both of her parents, Howie was not yet understanding what was ahead, and his father knew it. "I'm afraid your brother won't be able to find me. He'll keep looking, but he won't find me," he told Audrey.

Howie was unable to face the possibility of life without his father. During his visits, Howie spent much of his time watching television, reading a newspaper or staring blankly ahead. It was not unlike the previous six years when Howie would visit his father every Sunday at home. Howie always sat in an orange vinyl chair between his father, who always reclined on a gray couch, and the brown recliner that Julie had always sat in. Together, Howie and his father either watched television or read the local newspaper. Their relationship had been strained and volatile for as long as Howie could recall. They had little in common and both freely expressed their opinions. Their discussions frequently turned into arguments, followed by several days of not speaking to one another. His father had nicknamed him "Radical" as a teenager. Howie shared his father's name, his disappearing hairline and his height. He also shared his father's need for symmetry and order, never realizing that the harder he tried to not be like his father, the more he became like him.

Howie had adored his mother, but he was unable to relate to his father. He had grown bitter about their relationship, still saddened that his father never verbally expressed his love to him. The two found a common bond in their love of baseball, sitting in front of the television and watching hundreds of New York Mets' games together. While the games brought them together, it also forever divided them. As a child, Howie spent hours finding, organizing and admiring hundreds of baseball cards. He was immensely proud of his collection and knew someday that it would be valuable.

In 1969, when packing to move from New York to Florida, Howard sold several years worth of old newspapers to a recycling company to collect a few dollars for the move. Newspapers were bought by weight, and Howard needed more money than the few dozen pounds of newspapers would provide. So he slipped his son's baseball card collection in with the newspapers to increase the weight. While the deception bothered Howie, the disposing of his baseball card collection devastated him. He would never be able to forgive his father.

The time Howie spent with his father after his mother died was out of obligation to his mother. He was there because he knew his mother would have been disappointed if he turned his back on his father. Howard had become part of Howie's routine, and Howie did what he needed to abate the guilt.

During his visits with his father in the nursing home, Howie couldn't touch his father and he couldn't look into his eyes. He couldn't face what was happening. Their relationship was unresolved and, like his sister, he was about to lose his strongest connection to his mother. He would watch Audrey hold their father, but couldn't bear to get that close.

"Are you dying too?" Howard asked as Howie sat in a chair beside him one afternoon in the nursing home. Without hesitation, Howie said, "No, I don't think so, Dad." Howie looked puzzled by his father's question, and seemed sure that his father was losing his grip on reality. Howie's identity was tied up in his parents, and his father had worried for many years how his son would adjust after his parents were gone. A part of Howie was truly dying, and Howard knew it.

While I was concerned about the limited time Howie had left to connect with his father, I understood his inability to look into his father's eyes. Howard had begun to frighten me. It was not something I could understand or explain at the time, but I later came to realize that it was the intensity of his stare. He could see into me and it made me uncomfortable. A power had developed inside of him that I wasn't prepared to experience or attempt then to understand.

Six days before her father's death, Audrey went to see him, taking with her some freshly laundered clothes. Howard preferred that she wash his clothes rather than allow the nursing home staff to wash them. He said he was concerned they would lose them, but we knew the humility of having strangers launder his soiled clothing was too much for him. "I won't be needing those," he told Audrey, smiling. She sat down beside him and watched as his eyes tracked around the room.

"Is someone here with us?" she asked her father. He nodded. "I don't know how they get around with all of that on," he said, his eyes moving around the room. Although images of robe-clad spirits gliding through the room ran through her mind's eye, Audrey didn't ask.

He again asked if she would be okay. She tried to reassure him, nodding her head, "I'll be fine, Dad."

"I'll never find another one like you," he said to her.

"We'll be together again, Dad." She had thought little about whether they would actually be together again, but it seemed so true at that moment and such the right thing to say. The words brought another smile to his face as they sat together holding each other's hands. He motioned to her with his right hand, pointing to his lips. She leaned over and kissed him, and he drifted off to sleep.

She instinctively knew what to say and do to make him happy and comfortable. She was patient and understanding, never asking him to repeat himself or questioning his words when they made no sense to her. He was looking to her for peace and love.

Howard's need for sleep had continued, as had conversing in his sleep. His face had steadily taken on a generally happier look than it had two weeks earlier. The frowns had ceased. He had begun frequently tightening his eyes and face as we do when bright lights are suddenly shined in our eyes. The more we watched him, the more we wondered whether the heavens were opening for him, the light streaming into his eyes.

He had begun smiling more frequently.

It definitely wasn't sleep that he was experiencing. It was his transition. His spirit was moving to the other side and he was taking us along for part of the ride. We marveled at all that we were seeing and hearing. It had become such an incredible adventure.

It became more difficult to understand his words while awake and asleep. He had an increasingly difficult time expressing himself aloud. Occasionally, he spoke clearly enough for us to understand his words, but not to comprehend the meaning.

That evening, his eyes darted around the room as he witnessed visions still beyond our comprehension. After dinner, he asked Audrey for ice cream, and she left the room to retrieve a bowl of orange sherbet that she had stored in a freezer at the nurses' station down the hall.

Audrey left the room feeling worn and run down. When she was away from him, her heart quickly sank as she pondered the inevitable. Walking down the hall, she moved her feet slowly, trying to stop the clock and her father's death. At the nurses' station, Peggy sat in her usual spot by the counter, sorting plastic bags. As Audrey approached, Peggy stood up, lifted her head and began searching the area with her eyes. Peggy strained to see all of the faces around her, pausing briefly on each one, looking more determined with every passing second. When she reached Audrey's face, she stopped. She cocked her head slightly to the right and smiled, stretching her arms out to greet Audrey. Her eyes stayed fixed on Audrey's as Audrey approached. Audrey placed her hands on the counter in front of Peggy, and Peggy took Audrey's hands in hers. Peggy pulled them to her face, holding them against her cheeks.

"You feel warm against my face," Peggy said, bringing Audrey's hands to her mouth and kissing them.

Tears puddled in Audrey's eyes as she looked back into her mother's eyes. Peggy was, at least for that moment, gone. It was her mother standing before Audrey. She knew it. She could feel it. As quickly as the feelings had come, they were gone, and Peggy released her grip on Audrey's hands and sat back down in the chair, resuming her work with the plastic bags.

Each time during the next few days that I would approach the nurses' station with Audrey, Peggy would lift her head and search the faces, stopping at Audrey's when we were within her vision. When I approached alone, Peggy continued with her projects, never lifting her head. Their spirits had become connected.

After Audrey left her father's room to retrieve the sherbet, Howard looked up at the ceiling, turned to his son and asked, "Is that electricity I'm seeing up there?" His eyes were curious and intense as he stared above his bed. "I don't see anything, Dad," Howie said to his father, as the three of us stared at the ceiling. I didn't respond, wondering if Howard's failing eyesight was making him unable to see clearly.

As Howie prepared to leave, he leaned over to his father and said, "You know I love you, Dad."

Several nights earlier, Howard told Howie he loved him, crying as he explained how desperately he wanted to return home. Uncomfortable by the emotions, Howie left his father within minutes, failing to tell his father that he loved him. Howie had needed for decades to hear his father say the words, but he had trouble processing them once they had finally been said. Howard wouldn't say it to him again.

"I know," Howard said, looking up at his son.

That evening, after Howie left and as Audrey and I sat on either side of Howard's bed, Howard looked at her and quietly said, "It's time for me to say good-bye." Audrey reached over and took his left hand in hers, and I reached over for his right hand. As I took his hand in mine, he turned his head to look at me. I met his eyes with mine and we stared into each other. My fear had been replaced by warmth and love. I could feel the power of his soul, and I didn't want to ever let go of him or that feeling. I looked down at our hands and noticed that I was softy stroking his hand. He needed support as he made the most significant step of his life. I was finally comfortable providing it.

He turned back to Audrey and said, "I'll be watching over you." She couldn't speak, as her emotions rose into her throat. She smiled and nodded.

"We'll be counting on it," I told him, my eyes filling with tears and my voice cracking. He turned back to me and fixed his stare on a tear that had formed in my right eye. He followed it as it ran down my cheek and fell onto my arm. The first time he had seen me cry. He continued staring into my eyes, smiled and turned back to his daughter.

"I'll take good care of her," I said, as he

studied her face.

We sat quietly for a few moments, looking at each other. I wanted to ask him questions. I wanted to better understand what he was experiencing, where he was going, what he had already come to understand about his transition. But it wasn't about my needs. It was about his.

"I guess this will be written about in the paper," he said, breaking the silence, leaving us wondering what he was really saying. "I have to let go now."

He pulled his hands out of our firm grasps. He looked at Audrey and pointed to his lips. She leaned over and kissed him twice. When she tried a third time, he held up his right hand to stop her. She sat back down in the chair beside him and reached for his hand that lay by his side. He pulled his hand away, wrinkled his brow and shook his head from side to side. He truly did need to let go and he needed for us to let go too. As his eyes slowly closed, he raised both hands and waved good-bye. A smile came across his face as his eyelids shut.

Tears flowed from Audrey's eyes. I moved

around the bed and knelt on the floor by her chair. I put my right arm around her shoulders and pulled us close together. She began to cry more freely.

We sat together that evening, watching his labored breathing. His chest rose and fell, frequently pausing between breaths. Ten to 15 seconds would pass between some breaths, and I could feel my own heart skip as I wondered if he would resume his breathing. My breath began to stop with his, resuming only when his resumed.

Focused on Howard, I was unaware that my hand was stroking Audrey's head. I watched my fingers gently running through the hair along the back of her head. It was my hand but my sense of touch was gone. I felt nothing and whispered to her, "It's not my hand." Barely able to speak, she nodded with a look of complete understanding. "I know. It's my mother. I can feel my mother."

Rain pounded against the window beside his bed, and we could hear thunder in the distance. Shortly after he closed his eyes, he began mumbling. The smile remained on his face. He squinted more frequently as though he were continuing to protect his eyes from the light, yet the only light we saw filtered into the room from the hallway. We heard him greet Audrey's mother, his smile widening and his mouth moving to kiss her. He looked more at peace than we had seen him in a decade. His skin had taken on a fresh, smooth look, and the bruises that had covered his arms and legs had disappeared. The age spots on his face had faded away. He suddenly looked so young and so healthy. He truly resembled the young man in the black-and-white photo taken in Italy in 1945, his foot resting on airplane artillery as though he were in charge of the war. He looked comfortable and happy then, and he looked comfortable and happy now.

"Look at the beautiful apples, Jules," he said softly. He had been the only one who ever called his wife Jules. We wondered what they were seeing together. An apple orchard? The Garden of Eden? Whatever it was, the look on Howard's face revealed that it was beautiful and peaceful — utopia. His arms were by his sides, his right hand cupped as though he were holding Julie's left hand. This was no dream. His final journey to the other side had begun. He was leaving his human frame piece by piece, and we were still being allowed to walk with him part of the way.

We slept on air mattresses at the foot of his bed that night, not wanting to leave him or the feeling of peace and love that so inexplicably filled the room and us. I was asleep within minutes, but Audrey lay awake, staring at the ceiling and not letting herself sleep, fearing that she would miss her father calling out in the night. She tossed from side to side, turning at one point to face her father's bed. She lay motionless, fixated on what she was witnessing, reveling in a moment meant only for her eyes.

When I awoke early the next morning, Audrey tried to put into words what she had seen. "It was unbelievable," she told me quietly so as not to disturb her father. "Hovering above his bed near the ceiling was what I could describe only as an oval shaped cloud of active electrical current. It was like a miniature electrical storm. As I stared at it, it closed up and disappeared."

The cloud appeared twice more that night, and each time she stared at it, it quickly disappeared. "It felt as if the heavens had opened," she whispered.

It was the same electrical current that her father had described to Howie and me the night before. How fascinating, I thought, that he described it only to me and his son after Audrey had left the room, and that I never thought to say anything to her. How fascinating that I didn't witness it. It was then that I truly began to realize the magnitude of the meaning and purpose of all that was occurring around us. The forces at work were powerful and undeniable. Howard was shrouded in goodness, and Audrey was suddenly ready to help him move on to the next level.

That morning, we felt rested and rejuvenated. After a night on the same air mattresses in a tent, we always awoke stiff and achy. On this day, there were no sore muscles or tired joints. A source of positive energy was in the room that filled our bodies and minds.

Although Howard's speech had become difficult to understand, his awareness of his surroundings was becoming heightened to a level that I couldn't comprehend. After leaving Audrey alone with her father most of that day, I returned in the late afternoon. As I approached the door to his room and before I rounded the corner to enable him to see me, Howard turned toward Audrey and struggled to speak. "Jeff's here," he whispered.

I paused as I got to the doorway, hearing the hum of the machine pumping oxygen into his nose. The constant noise had initially annoyed me, but I had grown to appreciate that it filtered out so much noise from the hallway, offering a more tranquil, undisturbed setting in the room. I stood in the doorway, feeling unsure about entering the room, wondering whether Audrey needed more time alone with her father. I could see only Audrey from where I stood, and she whispered from across the room, "Come in. Dad knows you're here." As I approached his bed, Howard opened his eyes and started to smile. He stopped abruptly when his eyes reached mine.

"What's wrong?" he managed to ask.

"Nothing, except that it's really hot out." He continued staring at me, but was too weak to talk anymore. Before coming into the room, I had complained to one of the nursing home's administrators about the lack of compassion that I had observed in one of the nurses. The conversation had frustrated me, and after several minutes, I left his office, stopping along the way to clear my mind of the irritation. My frustration had, I thought, left me by the time I reached Howard's room.

Pondering Howard's question and his ability to see into me, I started to understand the significance of our eyes and vision. Howard had become able to gather much about us through our eyes, and we were able to learn much by looking into his. We take for granted so much that happens with our eyes, and I began to wonder how babies and animals know to look into our eyes when we speak. If they are reacting to our voices, they would look at our mouths. But, they look into our eyes, searching for enlightenment. I was beginning to understand that much occurs that we may see, but that our brains do not allow us to consciously recognize or understand. Until the time is right. The time appeared right for Howard.

As I stood at the foot of Howard's bed, he struggled to look around the room. His stare paused about a foot to my right at a level even with my head. I stared at him as he knitted his brow in what appeared to be an attempt to better understand what he was seeing. He glanced to the right to meet my eyes. He smiled and winked at me, knowing that I had been watching him. I was finally getting it, and he knew it.

As we stood outside his room that afternoon, I looked down the hall to see Conrad, his sneakers back on his feet and laces tied, heading in our direction. His movements were different this time, more deliberate. As I watched him from 15 feet away, I knew that he had a purpose; he had something to share with us. I didn't know how I knew it. I just knew it. Audrey and I stood motionless, waiting for him to make his way down the hall. He peddled his wheelchair to us, moving by me and stopping in front of Audrey. He reached his right hand out toward her, placing it gently on her folded arms. "It's been a lot of hard work," he said, staring into her eyes.

Her father couldn't communicate much verbally anymore, but he was still speaking to us. He wanted us to understand and he wanted us to get it. Looking into Conrad's eyes, we could see the enlightenment and understanding.

We slept in Howard's room again that night, absorbing all of the feelings that we could. We both knew that when his transition was complete, everything would change. We weren't quite ready for that change; we wanted to revel in this moment.

We were in and out of Howard's room throughout the next day, just three days before he died. As Audrey, her brother and I stood in the hallway outside their father's door, we saw The Clapper making her way down the hall in her wheelchair, moving the chair with her feet in the same way that Conrad did. As she approached, a smile spread across her face, revealing her gums and tongue. For the first time, Audrey and I looked into her eyes, seeing the same recognition that we had seen in Conrad's eyes. We were no longer afraid. Rather, we felt a sense of comfort being near her. It was an inexplicable change.

"Look at me," she said, her eyes fixed on Howie. His eyes wandered around the hallway, not stopping on The Clapper. "Look at me," she said again, in a more determined tone. She turned to me and Audrey and smiled. Looking back at Howie, her tone grew stronger as she said, "Look into my eyes." Howie looked in her direction, but was unable to look directly into her eyes. "I said, look into my eyes!"

"Okay, I'm looking. Now what?" he responded, exasperated.

"I want you to look into my eyes," she told him again, and he finally obliged her.

"Now, look at my head," she said. Her gray hair was pulled tightly back into a pony tail. "You see, I'm bald just like you." She looked back at me and Audrey and grinned. The woman was most definitely not bald. But Howie was nearing it. Despite his best efforts to conceal it, Howie had inherited his father's hairline.

Howie still hadn't gotten it. Howard needed his son to look into his eyes. He needed to make sure his son would be okay, and also needed to help enlighten him. He needed Howie to get it. Not looking into his father's eyes had left Howie shortchanged. He wasn't connecting to his father's transition and he wasn't understanding the greater meaning around him.

The Clapper resumed her trip down the hall. As she passed by us, she looked at me and said, "Do you want to come with me?"

"I'm sorry, I can't," I told her.

"I know. You've got to stay here and take care of her," she said, pointing at Audrey.

"Yes, I do."

As we had come to understand more and more about Howard and his transition, I had wanted and needed to understand even more. None of it was enough for me. I wanted to take the next step, to see a little more. I wasn't satisfied with what we had been given, and, yes, I did want to go with him. But the old woman was right. I needed to take care of my wife.

Later that afternoon, we passed The Clapper parked in her wheelchair by the nurses' station. Upon seeing me, she stretched her arms out and said, "I understand you."

"I know you do," I said, locking on her eyes. The understanding she had of me was clear. It was as though we had known each other for a lifetime.

A Work in Progress

Two days before Howard's death, I spent about an hour alone with him, sitting by his bed watching him, marveling at the man he had become. His verbal communication had become extremely limited. This time, I spoke and hoped he was listening.

"You've been very brave," I whispered, leaning closer to him. "It's been a very brave battle. It's been good for Audrey to spend all of this time with you. It's been good for her."

"Ya," he muttered softly, unable to open his eyes.

I closed my eyes and prayed that the suffering would end soon for him and Audrey. As I rested my head on the back of the chair, my mind wandered back nearly a decade to when I was first getting to know my future in-laws. Early on in our relationship they taught me to play Pinochle, spending hours perfecting the game. Julie had always sat to my right and Audrey to my left as the four of us paired off. In her 70s for much of the time I knew her, Julie was a petite and delicate woman. She spoke infrequently, but conveyed great love in her dark brown eyes. She would reach up to kiss my cheek every time I saw her, our eyeglasses knocking together more times than not. Her reaction still makes me smile; after our glasses touched, she would smile, reach up to adjust hers and say, "Oh, our glasses clinked." She always referred to me as her "little friend" with a tone of affection that has stayed with me to this day.

Coming to our home for dinner was an adventure for her, and she always wore her favorite outfit — pastel dress slacks, a print blouse and a tiny silver bicycle pin positioned on her blouse just below her right shoulder. After dinner, she frequently sat in a wooden Lincoln rocker in the corner of our family room, slowly rocking herself to sleep. She never intended to sleep, and I loved watching her sit in that chair dozing off, her sneakers touching the floor only when the chair rocked forward. She looked so comfortable and so much at peace. I had hoped that it was true that daughters turn into their mothers.

I lifted my head from the chair and opened my eyes to watch Howard as he lay motionless in front of me. His eyes were closed and he was mumbling words that I couldn't comprehend, no matter how hard I strained or how close I leaned into him.

I was amazed at how strong he looked. His stomach was flat and his chest looked toned and muscular. I strived to look so fit.

When I first met him nine years earlier, he was quiet and polite. He was a gentle man who immediately showed respect for me. I had feared that first meeting. I expected to spend the evening before a jury tasked with determining whether I was worthy of Audrey. It had been such a significant step for her. Like her father, Audrey was deeply private, sharing few of the intimate details of her life, even with her close family. She had been reluctant to tell them about her divorce in 1991 and was concerned about them knowing there was someone new in her life, especially someone nearly 13 years younger than her. To take me to meet her parents was big. She planned to be with me for the duration.

We drank Schlitz beer and ate fried shrimp on TV trays in the living room of their one-story concrete block home. The conversation focused on the food, the weather and our families. I had made myself uncomfortable as I wondered whether they had done the math. Their daughter was about to turn 41 and I was 28. Did they know my age? Did they think about it? Did they care?

"My parents live in Michigan, my brother and his family live in Vermont, and I have grandparents in Arizona and upstate New York," I explained. "But I grew up in Atlanta and Canada." Howard had already looked surprised with the four states, and his eyebrows drew further up his head when I mentioned Canada. He focused his attention on New York, the one area of North America that he was familiar with.

"Whereabouts in New York?" he asked. He had heard of Corning, but wasn't exactly sure where it was located. We moved on to talk about his family's roots throughout New York City's boroughs — a word I hadn't been familiar with until that night.

After dinner, he took us into their den — a small room between their bedroom and kitchen that was packed full of furniture. A large TV console sat against one wall, a stereo sat against another, a desk sat against another and Howard's 1974 electric Gulbransen organ sat against another. White shades covered the windows and drapes covered the shades, eliminating any possibility that natural light could enter the room. Howard seated himself at the wooden bench in front of the organ, a small florescent lamp hovering over his sheet music providing the only light. Julie, Audrey and I sat on small, unsteady wooden chairs, facing Howard's back. He started by playing *It Had To Be You*, *Are You Lonesome Tonight* and then *I Just Called to Say I Love You*, pausing long enough between songs to allow us time to clap.

I watched his wife and daughter marvel at his talent. I marveled at his talent. Music had always been an important part of his life and, while I didn't know it at the time, for him to share it with me that first night meant that I had been accepted.

Howard's love of music had been with him all of his life. In the 1930s, when he was a teenager, he decided to take piano lessons at the U.S. School of Music in New York City. He paid $2 for each lesson and was so committed to learning how to play the piano that even when his fingers were bandaged from a ringworm infection, he refused to miss a lesson.

He later wrote some of his own music and taught himself to play the guitar, harmonica, accordion and organ. He shared his talents with his family and other Air Force draftees during the war. In the Air Force's 487th Bombardment Squadron's album, published as "the clouds of World War II are still darkening the world," a caption under a picture of him reads, "He loves to tickle the ivories and what sweet sounds come forth."

He continued to play for nearly five decades after returning from the war, bringing his wife and three children together many evenings after dinner. *Glow Worm*, a fast-paced medley, was one of his more challenging pieces and one that Howie always requested as a child, asking his father to play "wiggle worm." The family would enjoy the request as much as hearing the song. After Julie's death, Howard no longer found pleasure in his music, and his playing waned.

Although conversations throughout our relationship never reached much beyond the weather, current events or the food that we gathered to share, I could feel his appreciation of me early in our relationship. I could feel the bond that grew quickly between us. He loved to try to teach me his favorite toast, which I could never memorize and that I actually never wanted to memorize because he loved to recite it to us at each dinner. As he raised his glass of beer, he would first pause to recite the toast in his head, and then would say it aloud. He would smile proudly afterwards, pleased that he had remembered it for so many years.

Howard had been bald with a thin white fringe around the sides and back of his head for the entire time that I had known him. He had looked the same for the first three years, but aged rapidly during the last six. The slowing of his heart and his lack of interest in food had shaved 30 pounds from his already slim 6-foot frame, leaving him looking frail and sunken.

We wondered what had kept him going those years after he lost his wife and his will to live. He had never planned to survive her. That was not the way he had thought it all out. He would go first and she would be left. After all, she was better able to care for herself. She had cared for their family all of those years.

But there was a different plan for them. There was a different plan for all of us.

Julie was the only one aware that the plan was not to be as Howard imagined it, telling her sister, Helen, one afternoon six months before Julie's death that she worried about whether Howard would be able to care for himself after she died. Her concern was obviously well placed. It may have come from knowing that throughout their 48 years of marriage, she had done all of the cooking and cleaning, leaving Howard with little experience in taking care of a house or his own basic needs. He consulted her on every decision.

It was a common scenario among their generation — Howard was to have the only career and be in charge of the family, and Julie would be responsible for raising the children and running the house. Julie's father had maintained such a role, and she was taught as a child that women were on Earth to be dutiful wives and mothers and were to maintain the peace and harmony in their homes. Julie's father had been a stern man who, by all accounts, was emotionally abusive to her, leaving her unsure of herself. While she grew into a considerate and loving woman, her quiet demeanor revealed a difficult past.

While the division of duty in their relationship was clearly defined by history, Howard wouldn't be able to fulfill his role.

Howard and Julie had been inseparable from their first meeting in April 1946, after Howard returned home from a four-year tour of duty in Italy as an Air Force mechanic. Ritchie Bahm, a friend he met in boot camp, had asked Howard to join him in New Hampshire to meet his sister after they were both discharged. Howard married the sister six months later in a small ceremony in Brooklyn, nine of their closest relatives with them. Like many newlyweds of that era, they honeymooned at Niagara Falls.

After they married, Howard and Julie moved to Indian River City, Florida, a rural community along Florida's central east coast that offered less expensive living and warmer weather than the Northeast. To them, it seemed a good place to start their lives together. Ritchie joined them, and Howard and Ritchie opened a woodworking business in 1948 where they made custom kitchen cabinets. Howard and Julie lived in a two-bedroom house attached to the business, and Ritchie slept in a bedroom connected to another part of the shop. The business thrived and life was good. Howard and Julie became the parents of a girl and two boys.

Howard was a stern father who taught his

children manners and respect for others, without ever raising a hand to them. His children and wife learned early on that their father's darker, brooding side required that they work to keep harmony in the family. His mood swings would shut down the family for hours and days at a time as they quietly waited for their gentle husband and father to re-emerge.

He controlled his family and they yielded to his needs, no matter how difficult their sacrifices. For Audrey, it was all about focusing on the good and forgetting the bad. It wasn't until after her father died that she shared the story of Bonnie, the apple pancake-loving golden blonde Labrador puppy mix that the family had picked out at an animal shelter 36 years earlier. Audrey and her brothers adored Bonnie, and her energy kept them running after her throughout the house. For the kids, it was the most exciting thing that had ever happened to them.

Bonnie developed an affinity for chewing the large braided rug that covered their living room floor. They struggled to train her not to chew the rug, but boredom often set in when she was alone. Howard insisted she be kept in the kitchen overnight, and he separated her from the rest of the house with a low gate in the kitchen doorway, which she quickly learned to climb over. Frustrated with the dog, Howard loaded her and the rest of his family into their light blue Ford Fairlane to return Bonnie to the animal shelter just three months after bringing her home. Audrey and her brothers were nearly hysterical with grief, fearing that Bonnie would be destroyed if no one adopted her.

They left Bonnie at the animal shelter, and for that brief moment, sitting behind her father in the car, Audrey had nothing but contempt for him. She found it within herself to hate her father. Sitting in the front seat with her husband, Julie was quiet, knowing that she was required to support her husband, no matter how difficult it was.

Howard drove his family to Woolworth's and told Audrey and her brothers that he would buy them each one gift of their choosing. He explained that he wanted to do something to help them feel better, but it likely was more about helping himself feel better. Audrey went to the craft section and chose the makings for wall hangings that she later made and gave to her parents. It is an event that Audrey recalls matter of factly. She had developed an amazing capacity to move on, to not distress over what many would consider injustices. She didn't waste her time or energy on the negative.

It wasn't that Howard disliked animals. After all, he had adored Caruso, a yellow canary that had lived in a silver cage hanging by their dining room window. Howard was so attached to Caruso, whom a neighbor had given to him in 1962, that when Caruso died in 1966, Howard couldn't dispose of him. Instead, he placed Caruso in a small box and stored him in the basement.

Animals generally threatened Howard's need for order and symmetry. Caruso lived in a cage, but dogs like Bonnie couldn't be controlled. Howard was obsessive about order, insisting that decorations be evenly aligned with all corners of the tables they sat on. He was so precise that he would use a ruler to draw lines inside greeting cards so that his writing would be linear. He was the neatest and most orderly of his seven siblings, his mother not daring to put his laundry away when he was a child for fear she would put it in the wrong place.

His standards for his own children were as high as those he placed on himself. Poor table manners and improper grammar were unacceptable in his house. His intellect had advanced him two grades in elementary school, and he boasted to his children when correcting their grammar that he had won numerous English medals as a child.

With such a tremendous focus on order and excelling, the frustration and disappointment that would come from Howard's inability to control all aspects of his own life seemed almost inevitable.

Back surgeries to repair a herniated disk in 1958 incapacitated him long enough that he and Ritchie were forced to close their business. Not having much money saved or a means to earn any, Howard retreated to his widowed mother in Queens, New York, moving his family into her cold, dark basement. His mother had become a bitter old woman who wanted little to do with her son or his family, locking them outside some days and refusing to turn on the heat in the basement that was their home for seven months. She forbade them to be in the rest of her house, forcing them to use a portable toilet in the basement instead of the bathroom upstairs. Howard had to ration toilet paper by the square for his family, never allowing more than four squares to be used at any one time.

Howard was not the man his mother had wanted him to become. She had been unhappy with him from the moment he returned from the war, when he focused his attention on Julie.

Several months after returning to the states, Howard's mother wrote in a letter to him: "Well, Howard, I was glad to receive the Mother's Day card but I surely thought I would be seeing you. If you recall a letter you wrote overseas, you stated that you hoped you would be home for next Mother's Day, which I thought could have been possible." Howard's mother was not happy about the new love that he had found in his life. She resented being replaced.

Unable to resolve the conflicts with his mother, Howard moved his family out of his mother's basement and into his sister's home on Long Island, where she, her husband and four children welcomed them as part of their family.

It took him a decade to regain his health and mobility, which allowed Howard and Ritchie to begin planning a new carpentry business that they would open in Florida in the fall of 1969. Stopping by his mother's house to say good-bye before returning to Florida, Howard was met by the same cold, bitter woman. She remained in the doorway and refused to say good-bye to him or his family. As Howard recounted the scene to his sister later that evening, it became the first time that Howie saw his father cry.

For Howard and Julie, it was now time to move on. Plans for the business were made. It would be like the one that had been so successful 11 years earlier. Howard and Ritchie worked well together and got along even better as friends. It was a rare relationship for Howard. He didn't develop friendships easily. He expected so much of people that it was difficult to meet his standards. He didn't waste his time on people who couldn't.

Moving back to Florida would be Howard's opportunity to rebuild the lives of those closest to him. He had a plan again.

Several weeks before they were to begin their work together again, 53-year-old Ritchie died of a heart attack. Howard and Julie were devastated. The business plans were canceled, and Howard never worked again. Two heart attacks weakened and demoralized him. He felt like a victim. Howard and Julie had already returned to Florida with their three children, and Howard relied on the government and his family to provide for them for the next 31 years.

Becoming a disappointment to himself, Howard shifted his attention to his family, working to ensure that they did not disappoint themselves or him.

As the youngest, Steven felt the greatest

pressure. In his early 20s, he began cashing forged checks. Those misdemeanor crimes turned into felonies as he wrote checks for increasingly larger amounts. He began spending his life in and out of jail. Early on, he wrote letters from jail to his parents demanding money and gifts. They blamed themselves for his problems, and gladly sent him everything he demanded. While he was in jail, his parents spent their days running errands for him, spending what little money they had on money orders that enabled him to buy candy and sandwiches. When he got out of jail, he would disappear for several years at a time. When he turned 30, his heartbroken mother sent a birthday card to the last address that she had for him, having written, "Dear Steven, how are you? We hope you are well. We haven't heard from you in a long time, we hope everything is okay. We have been trying to contact you with no luck. Will you please drop us a line or a post card or call and let us know how you are. Happy birthday and we hope you enjoy it. Take care and please write. All our love, Mom and Dad." The birthday card came back to her stamped "undeliverable." She placed the card in her dresser under her clothes, never reopening the envelope.

Several years later, Steven re-emerged as though he had only been gone for a couple of days, offering no explanation as to where he had been. His parents were so grateful to have him back in their lives that they didn't press him for answers. He stayed briefly and spoke to his parents for the last time on Easter in 1991. His father rarely spoke of him again. As the years went on, Howard told people he had only two children. His mother longed to see Steven before she died, but it wasn't part of the plan.

A nurse walked into the room, fast-forwarding me back to the present. I lifted my head from the chair to watch her quietly move about the darkened room, glancing at me and watching Howard. She had told us how amazed she had been with all that he allowed us to see and hear as he made his transition, noting that she had never seen someone share so much in the more than 20 years that she had

been a nurse.
     We had been blessed.

To God

The following day, Howard could no longer mutter any words to us. Audrey spent the day caressing his head, arms and hands. His breathing was labored and his chest was filling with fluid. The phlegm rattled as he took in each breath, prompting me to frequently clear my own throat. A nurse referred to it as the death rattle because the sounds were usually closely followed by death. She had warned us that it would happen, but I was unprepared for the chill that it gave me to hear. Perhaps the chill came from knowing what was next. I had wondered how we would know it when we heard it.

It was impossible to miss.

We sat beside him, recounting memories of

years before, following Joellen's lead. Joellen had come from Hospice to sit with Howard and to help get us used to the idea that he would soon be moving on. As she stood beside him, holding the rail of his bed, her words appeared to soothe him. His face looked relaxed and he was calm, turning his head slightly toward her as she spoke.

As we reminded him of the Pinochle games that we had played and the holiday dinners that we had shared, the smiles that crept so slightly across his face confirmed what we had known all along — his control over his body had diminished, but his hearing and understanding were fine. He was still keenly aware of all that was occurring around and to him.

Audrey asked him about returning home. Understanding the concept of going home had been one of the most difficult things for us. Every time Howard had told us that he was ready to go home, we wondered why he would want to return to living alone, especially in the dark and dingy house that seemed so depressing to us. We had assumed that he feared losing the connection to Julie that he had felt so strongly in their home.

This time, though, our understanding allowed Audrey to ask, "Do you want to go home and be with the family?" Howard nodded. It was exactly what he wanted, to be in his real home with his family. His house as we knew it had nothing at all to do with going home.

He occasionally opened his eyes for brief periods, looking around the room as he did.

Later that afternoon, his son sat in a chair beside him. He put his hand on his father's, and his father opened his eyes, looking deeply into his son's eyes. As Howie held his father's hand, caressing it with his, they were silent. He sat with him much of the day, holding his father as he had watched his sister do for weeks. He was getting more comfortable and at ease. The television was off and the newspaper was on the floor.

That night, we slept at home, encouraged to leave by nurses who told us Howard could live one day or 10 days. There was no way to know. His heartbeat and blood pressure were strong. He wasn't quite ready to go.

Audrey awoke the next morning dreading the day ahead. She knew it was time and she knew this would be the day. She dressed and went to visit her father, wondering if he would be able to respond to her or even know that she was there.

As she sat beside her father in what became the few hours before he died, she became aware that they were not alone in the room. She felt familiarity. She felt love. She felt family.

"They're here, aren't they Dad?" she asked her father. "They're here to take you home."

A smile spread across his face that let her know that they were, indeed, there, and that they were planning to take him home soon. "It's okay to go, Dad. Really." He smiled again, gripping her hand so tightly that she wondered where the strength came from. He had barely eaten in three weeks, was unable to speak or open his eyes, yet he was able to hold her more tightly than he had in years.

She sat next to him, holding him, waiting with him.

At 3 p.m., Audrey stepped into the hallway outside her father's room to stretch her legs. She watched as Conrad peddled his wheelchair up to Howard's door. He stretched an arm out and touched my father-in-law's name tag on the wall next to the door to his room.

"To God," he said, resting his fingers for a moment on the name tag. He withdrew his hand, turned the wheelchair with his feet away from the wall and resumed peddling himself down the hallway.

Nearly two hours later, Howard's work was complete. It was time for him to go home.

Howard had waited until after Audrey left his room again. He had already shared so much with her, and now, this private moment would be shared only with his son. Howie watched as his father drew his last breath. He watched as the color drained from his father's face.

Audrey, Howie and I gathered in a waiting area until Howard's body was removed from the nursing home. Tears streamed down Audrey's cheeks. I held Audrey's shoulders as we walked by the nurse's station to leave the nursing home for the last time. There sat Peggy, her body and head jerking up as she sensed Audrey's presence. She quickly found Audrey's eyes and extended her arms to her. As Audrey approached the counter that separated them, she reached her arms out to Peggy, and Peggy cupped Audrey's hands in hers.

"Why so sad?" Peggy asked.

"My Dad's gone," Audrey told her.

Peggy's eyes conveyed that she was well aware that Howard was gone — that wasn't what she was asking. Her question was rhetorical. How could Audrey be so sad when she now so clearly understood that her father was finally home with her mother?

A nurse reached for Peggy's shoulders, trying to gently pull her from Audrey and return her to the chair that she had been sitting in.

"Come on Peggy, leave her alone," the nurse softly pleaded.

Peggy maintained her grip on Audrey's hands and they stared into each other.

"No, please, it's okay," I assured the nurse,

prompting her to release Peggy's shoulders.

The nurse and I stood motionless watching Peggy and Audrey linked together. It was a moment that left Audrey feeling great comfort. Peggy slowly released Audrey's hands, sat back down and dropped her eyes to the desk in front of her.

As we resumed our walk down the hallway and I guided Audrey toward the two glass doors leading to the parking lot, I saw Conrad approaching us. Stopping two feet in front of Audrey, Conrad cocked his head and smiled. "You've been a very good daughter," he told her, the words barely out of his mouth when he resumed his trip down the hall. More comforting words. Whether they actually came from Conrad or whether he was simply the messenger used to deliver them, we didn't know. It didn't matter.

That night, Audrey, Howie and I lifted our glasses of Chardonnay together and I recited Howard's toast, "Here's to you as good as you are, and to me as bad as I am. But, as good as you are and as bad as I am, I'm as good as you are as bad as I am."

We laughed and cried simultaneously.

Thursday

The next day, we went into his house. It was a Thursday.

≈

Returning Home

Time to Refocus

As the casket with Howard's body and Julie's ashes was raised 12 feet off the ground and slid into the dark, vacant crevasse on the fifth level of the mausoleum, I held Audrey's shoulders, watching and waiting with her family. We stood silently, each with our own thoughts. Each with our own memories.

As the sun shone down on us, I clearly imagined Howard's body in the casket, lying peacefully in the gray slacks, short-sleeved pale green shirt and navy cardigan sweater that Audrey and I had chosen for him. That navy cardigan. Howard had worn that sweater nearly every day that I had seen him in the nursing home before the hospital gown and robe had become his complete wardrobe. I recalled him struggling to walk us to our car after each visit, his wooden cane in his right hand and his daughter's hand in his left. He always wore that navy cardigan.

Audrey and I had selected his clothes carefully the previous day, making sure that his body was dressed as simply in death as it had been in life. We decided there would be no tie, no jacket. He would be dressed in the clothes that he had been comfortable wearing. We matched everything with that navy sweater. The navy sweater had to be with him. It had become such a significant part of him. More importantly, it had become such a significant part of our memories of him. We needed to continue remembering him wearing that sweater.

Audrey and I spent much time reflecting at the cemetery, marveling at all that had happened during the previous few weeks and wondering what lay ahead. Our future looked much different now. We suddenly had new choices to make. We could most easily return to our lives and our routines, feeling somewhat more enriched from the experiences that we had shared. Or we could refocus.

It appeared time to refocus.

The day had taken on special meaning. It wasn't just the day we tied up the loose ends of her parents' and grandparents' lives. It happened to be Good Friday. Another reminder that we shouldn't, that we couldn't, make the easy choice to return to our old lives and routines. We must learn the purpose, our purpose.

Audrey and I spent the next several days reflecting, talking, speculating, mourning and rejoicing. We discussed issues that we had never before discussed, issues that we had never before felt were important enough to discuss. We talked about God, about religion, about life and about death. We longed for the spiritual connection that had been so strong, so present, in Howard's room.

We spent time together and we spent time alone. I spent part of that Easter weekend working in our yard. It was time that allowed my mind and spirit to wander. My work was arbitrary, as I wandered around trimming shrubs and pulling weeds. I was unfocused on my tasks, yet my mind was clearly focused, as I tried to better understand. I wanted to make sure that I really got it. The thorns that stuck into my fingers brought me back momentarily. I continued on, my fingers becoming more sore and inflamed as my mind remained focused on my father-in-law. I looked down and saw the tiny thorns imbedded under the skin of both hands. A crown of thorns. I was actually trimming the one crown of thorns bush in our yard. I stood motionless as it all began to connect. It was Easter Sunday and I was trimming a crown of thorns. It was one of those moments that are so significant that we never forget them.

It was most definitely time to refocus.

I worked unsuccessfully to remove the thorns from my hands that afternoon, carrying them with me for several days. Every time I used my hands, I was reminded. I was reminded to think and to work to understand. I had been focusing all of my appreciation and wonderment on Howard for teaching us so much, for giving us so much. But I came to understand that Howard was an instrument used to teach us. The powers that worked through him were far greater than any human being.

Returning to work the day after Easter, the annoyance of rush hour traffic was gone. I looked at the drivers in cars around me as we all inched our way through a toll plaza on the East-West Expressway leading into downtown Orlando. Some sat gripping their steering wheels while others scanned in desperation for a faster way around the thousands of cars in front of them. "I wonder if they get it, if they really get it," I said aloud. Obstacles that had seemed so immense to me only weeks earlier were inconsequential. I was refocusing. I was getting perspective.

Audrey and I waited two weeks before going back into her parents' house. It was time to begin cleaning out a half century's accumulation. She first wanted to gather her mother's jewelry. She looked for her mother's wedding ring and the small bicycle pin. She came across a white apron dotted with pink roses that she had made for her mother 40 years earlier. It was neatly folded in the middle drawer of her mother's dresser. Audrey sat on the edge of her parents' queen-sized bed, unfolded the apron and held it to her cheek, longing to be holding her mother instead. Audrey had been nine when she made the apron for her mother. She stitched it by hand, attaching pink trim unevenly around the entire apron. It was a treasure her mother kept close to her.

These memories had been off-limits while Howard had been alive. He had been so fearful of doing anything that would end Julie's visits after her death.

Searching through her mother's dresser, Audrey came across her mother's gold watch. Time for the watch had stopped at 4:47, the same moment that Howie saw his father take his last breath.

During the next few weeks as we sorted through her parents' lives, Audrey came to better understand them and their relationship. Hidden in the bottom of her father's dresser, she came across books that offered couples insight into how to maintain complete and loving relationships. Stuffed in an old Marvel hosiery box lay all of the memories of their wedding and honeymoon. Neatly packed together in the box were greeting cards, road maps of New England, New York and Quebec, 75 cents in Canadian coins, and postcards from Montreal, Ausable Chasm and Glens Falls — all of the places they visited before reaching Niagara Falls. There were birthday, Christmas and Easter greeting cards that spanned the first few years of their marriage. Audrey found dozens of other cards and notes to each other from throughout their lives together, each expressing a heartfelt message of devotion and love.

She found simple notes that her father had written to her mother after her mother's death, when he left sustenance for his wife. "Julie, applesauce for you, love, Howard," read one note. He remained devoted to her after her death, ensuring that her needs as he understood them were met.

Audrey had always known that her parents were close, but had never before grasped the depth of their feelings for one another. She now truly understood her father's devastation after her mother's death. She understood why he left Julie's clothes undisturbed. She understood why her mother had come back for him. She understood that her mother's mission, at least in part, was to watch over Howard. She understood why her parents traveled home together holding each other's hand the night he said good-bye to us in the nursing home. They were meant to be together. It was part of the plan.

Audrey smiled as she imagined the day she and I would travel together hand in hand on our way home. We, too, were meant to be together. We both felt it and we both knew it.

"I'm not afraid," she said to me. "I'm not afraid to die. This sounds weird and I don't mean to sound like I want to die, but I'm actually looking forward to it."

They were words I had thought to myself and feared would sound bizarre if I said them aloud.

They didn't sound bizarre hearing Audrey say them.

How could we be afraid now?

Understanding Howard's journey home filled us with anticipation.

Returning Home

What It's All About

The year following our journey was one of much contemplation. Audrey and I discussed all that had happened to and around us, trying to better understand where it took us and where it might yet take us. The purpose churned through our thoughts as we paused for the first time in our lives to really consider a bigger picture.

"I don't understand what it's all been about, but I guess I'll find out." While I thought about many of Howard's statements after his death, that one continued to come back to me as I reflected on the day that I hoped to learn the answers to so many seemingly unanswerable questions.

Howard's statement came to define so

much of our thoughts and discussions. The peace with which his spirit departed his body suggested that he did, indeed, find out what it had all been about.

Our minds, I have decided, are not meant to truly grasp everything around us. Our brains have been specifically wired to grasp much, but not everything. Such is the case with the question of who created God. If God created us, then something or someone must have created God. But then, who created God's creator? We're taught that God just is and always was. But how can that be possible? We're just not equipped to understand. We're not yet meant to understand.

Should too many answers be available to us, the physical and spiritual worlds would become one. Then where would our effort be? While I certainly have come to understand that our meaning and purpose are based on love and goodness, I have yet to truly understand why we're here. Why do we not simply learn these things in the spiritual world? Why do they not just exist for all of us? Why the need for this world at all?

It had always been so easy to say that I believed in God. There was never a time that I can recall that I didn't believe in God. There were certainly times when I questioned why God was not there at that moment during a time of difficulty to support me. And it was during those times that I questioned His very existence. But, I never didn't believe in Him.

At the same time, the spiritual world was rarely a conscious part of my life. It was always there for me, but nothing that I spent much time thinking about.

Until Howard's death.

The time that Audrey and her father spent together in the weeks before he died had so much purpose. It clearly was to bring the two of them closer together and to allow them to connect more than they ever had. Developing that connection was certainly not the only purpose in those final few weeks, but it was a significant part of it.

Seeing Howard spend so much time working through his life in the nursing home, it was clear that he sorted through most every event that he had experienced, looking so enlightened at times, and so perplexed at others. I believe it's a stage that we will all go through in our transition to the other side, whether it be in a coma or asleep, or whether it be after our spirits have left our bodies. For some, perhaps it's rapid. For others, it may take longer. I trust that the harder we work here to be good to our friends, family and people whom we pass in our lives, the easier that our transitions will be.

During the year after Howard's death, I spent much time thinking about the people whom I have known, and pondered whether I had always treated them as well as I should have. Have I done or said things that I would be ashamed of during my transition? Yes, of course I have.

I imagine the transition to be similar to the trial in the movie, *Defending Your Life*. In the movie, after people die, they visit Judgment City, where a trial with prosecutors and defense attorneys is held. The trial focuses on people's lives and how they dealt with fear. While it's a comedic look at the transition, I imagine that the premise is similar to what really occurs. There may be no trial-like atmosphere, but Howard showed us that there most certainly is a replay of our lives that offers us an opportunity to better understand how we've impacted other people.

There are magnificent forces at work helping us along the way in this life when we ask for help, and when we don't. There are also strong forces working against our enlightenment, forces that Audrey and I have both become much more tuned into since becoming more enlightened and connected to the spiritual world.

Those negative forces became most evident during Howard's final few weeks and in the following year. The more we understood the goodness that we were learning about, the stronger the negative forces became. It started with lights coming on when we hadn't turned them on, leaving us wondering which of us had turned them on and forgotten.

One night, I awoke from a deep sleep to hear the door knob to our bedroom jiggling as though someone were trying to get in. Another night I awoke feeling a presence in our bedroom. As I lay there looking around the room, I watched a mist form in the corner of the room. It hovered and then darted to the other side and disappeared. I wondered if I was hallucinating, but knew that I was too clear-thinking for any of what I was experiencing to not be real. I was enveloped in feelings of fear and dread.

There were many nights when both Audrey and I awoke at the same time in the middle of the night, both of us terrified by a presence in our bedroom. There was nothing that we could see, but the feeling was undeniable. We were not alone, and whatever was there with us was not good. It reminded Audrey of one evening early in her father's transition when he complained that, "They keep picking at me. They won't leave me alone." As he spoke, he looked around his body, the unhappiness on his face revealing that whatever was picking at him was not a welcome sight or experience.

Audrey and I began praying together when we awoke feeling negative energy in our bedroom.

There were many evenings when we

watched our two cats awaken simultaneously from deep sleeps, jerk their heads and stare at the same wall. In unison, they would follow movement across the room, sometimes hissing with the hair standing up on their backs. Just as Howard was clearly seeing people in the nursing home whom we could not see, our pets appear somehow more connected than our brains allow us to be.

Although it took months, the horrors in the middle of the night ended. Prayer and faith carried us far.

The unusual experiences did not end when the negative forces moved on.

One evening while lying on a couch in our family room watching television, Audrey felt something brush by her check. As she turned to focus on it, she saw nothing. But the smell of her father suddenly filled the air around her. While driving alone in her car, Audrey has been jolted by the overwhelming aroma of her father on many occasions. The smells are brief, but powerful.

It's likely that there had been spirits around us long before Howard died, but we were not enlightened enough to recognize or feel them. I've thought back on all of the times when I've been uncomfortable for no known reason, or felt something was wrong, but didn't know what it was. There were times when I inexplicably got goose bumps, and times when the hair on the back of my neck stood up. So many times, I had no idea why these things were happening. Inexplicable but legitimate reactions, whether I'm reacting to something that my eyes see and my brain can't process, or whether I'm reacting to some force around me that on some level I can feel.

It wasn't until I was explaining to my cousin four months after Howard's death that our experience was spiritual rather than religious that I first started to grasp that they were one and the same. "What's the difference?" she asked, trying to better understand. I tried to explain, but realized I didn't know myself. I turned to Audrey for help and neither of us could put it into words.

I had been so careful to not attach any religious connection to our experiences because religion had always felt hypocritical and intolerant to me. I didn't want our experience of love and enlightenment to be confused with fire and brimstone.

But what we experienced was spiritual, and it was religious at the same time. It was about love, forgiveness, kindness, faith and how we treat people.

It was about God.

It was about all of the things that religion and spirituality should always be about. It was about all of the things that our daily lives should always be about.

The experience when and after Howard died has, indeed, forever altered the way we look at the world and our lives. Our time here is brief, yet there's much to be accomplished before we move on. I spend much less time on wasted emotions like anger and hate. I work harder to avoid hurting other people's feelings, and I apologize when I realize that I fail and hurt them anyway. I express my appreciation and love for people in my life, and I try to reach out to those who hurt.

During that year after Howard's death, a brother, a baby and a husband of relatives and friends died tragically and unexpectedly. I found myself able for the first time in my life to offer words of love and encouragement. I knew the words to say because I understood more about how it all works. I grieved for the survivors, but tried to offer the hope that we would all be reunited some day.

I know that there has been much that I'll better understand when it comes time for my own transition. I know that I'll learn about times when I was unaware of the pain that I caused others. I'll learn about times when I failed to make the right choices. But I'm hopeful that by trying to always remember what I learned through my father-in-law that my life will be more enriched, while I'll also be better able to enrich the lives of others with whom I come into contact.

And now faith, hope, and love abide, these three;
and the greatest of these is love.
1 Corinthians 13:13

Afterword

lthough it has been only a little more than a year since my father's passing, he continues to have a daily influence on our lives. Sometimes, it's obvious revelations. Other times, it's much more subtle. But his presence is always felt.

Not in my wildest dreams would I have ever given thought to the fact that my father would have such a major impact on my life. I always adored him. I can recall that, as a small child, I would sit on his lap, not wanting the world to move forward beyond that place in time. He was by no means perfect. In fact, he was far from it. But no matter what the imperfections, our bond was undeniably strong.

What I most remember is the secrecy with

which he led his life, and how strikingly different it was from those final few weeks. As a family, we would discuss little. Our thoughts and feelings were to be kept to ourselves, which makes it even more remarkable to me that my father would come to share with us his final days of life here. Looking back, I would not change anything that brought us to this place. For me, it was worth the 50-year wait.

Today, as I stare at my father's wooden cane hanging in the back of my closet, I am still filled with many emotions. I am reminded of his struggle to maintain his independence, while never quite succeeding. I am reminded of the frustration he felt in surrendering that independence. I am reminded of our slow walks through the halls of the nursing home. But, most of all, I am reminded of him. I recall the day shortly after his passing that I saw the cane leaning against my closet door. It so vividly reminded me of the final scene in *Miracle on 34th Street*, a movie that he and I always watched together each Christmas. He was finally home.

In a daily spiritual devotional that I began

reading after my father made his transition, I recently came across a quote from the Bible that I thought captured my feelings. To verify that the reference was accurately quoted, I located a small Bible that I had found tucked away in a drawer in my mother's dresser. I opened the Bible to find a delicate and worn bookmark with a color drawing of Mary Magdalene kneeling before Jesus, her arms stretched out to him. Below them is the reference, "I am he that liveth." I found the bookmark already marking the very page that I was searching for.

The quote from Luke 8:16 reads, "No one lights a lamp and hides it in a jar or puts it under a bed. Instead, he puts it on a stand, so that those who come in can see the light."

My father is my connection to a life here and now, and a life everlasting. My appreciation goes beyond the written word, and my greatest wish is to one day be eternally reunited with my father and mother.

Thank you, Dad, for helping me to see the light.

Audrey Cole – June 2001

ISBN 141203854-5

9 781412 038546